SCIENCE FICTION IN THE MEDIA

BY JOHN HAMILTON

Visit us at

www.abdopublishing.com

Published by ABDO Publishing Company, 4940 Viking Drive, Suite 622, Edina, Minnesota 55435.
Copyright ©2007 by Abdo Consulting Group, Inc. International copyrights reserved in all countries.
No part of this book may be reproduced in any form without written permission from the publisher.
ABDO & Daughters™ is a trademark and logo of ABDO Publishing Company.

Printed in the United States.

Editor: Paul Joseph
Graphic Design: John Hamilton
Cover Design: Neil Klinepier
Cover Illustration: Hayden Christensen, Corbis
Interior Photos and Illustrations: p 1 scene from *The Deadly Mantis*, Getty Images; p 4 fan at science fiction convention, Corbis; p 5 *Amazing Stories* cover, Mary Evans Picture Library; p 6 *Flash Gordon* comic, courtesy King Features; p 7 comic books, Corbis; p 8 man with shotgun, Corbis; p 9 Orson Welles, Getty Images; p 10 promo poster for *Captain Video*, Getty Images; p 11 scene from *Tom Corbett— Space Cadet*, Getty Images; p 12 scene from *The Twilight Zone*, Getty Images; p 13 (top) cover of *Voyage to the Bottom of the Sea* DVD set, courtesy Twentieth Century Fox; p 13 (bottom) scene from *Lost in Space*, Corbis; p 14 cast of *Star Trek*, Getty Images; p 15 Gene Roddenberry, Corbis; p 16 *Star Trek* memorabilia, Getty Images; p 17 *Farscape* cast, courtesy Jim Henson Productions; p 18 Ray Harryhausen, Getty Images; p 19 *Flash Gordon* poster, Getty Images; p 20 (top) scene from *Proboscis*, courtesy Sparrow Media Group; p 20 (bottom) scene from *Godzilla*, Getty Images; p 21 George Lucas, Getty Images; p 22 scene from *Star Wars: Episode II*, Getty Images; p 23 cast of *Star Wars: Episode II*, Getty Images; p 24 *E.T.* poster, Getty Images; p 25 Steven Spielberg, Getty Images; p 26 (top) scene from *The Day After Tomorrow*, Corbis; p 26 (bottom) Ridley Scott, Corbis; p 27 (top) scene from *Aliens of the Deep*, Corbis; p 27 (bottom) James Cameron, Corbis; p 28 portrait of Don Maitz; p 29 *Heavy Time* ©1990 Don Maitz.

Library of Congress Cataloging-in-Publication Data

Hamilton, John, 1959-
    Science fiction in the media / John Hamilton.
        p. cm. -- (The world of science fiction)
    Includes index.
    ISBN-13: 978-1-59679-994-3
    ISBN-10: 1-59679-994-3
    1. Science fiction--History and criticism. I. Title. II. Series: Hamilton, John, 1959- World of science fiction.

    PN3433.5.H37 2007
    809.3'8762--dc22
                            2006016394

CONTENTS

Books and Magazines 4

Comics 6

Radio 8

Television 10

Science Fiction Films..18

Science Fiction Art 28

Glossary 30

Index..32

BOOKS AND MAGAZINES

In the beginning was the Word. The greatest science fiction—from early stories like Mary Shelly's *Frankenstein* and H. G. Wells' *The Time Machine*, to modern masterpieces like Dan Simmons' *Hyperion*—started as the printed word. Especially in the early days of the genre, at the dawn of the 20th century, people got their dose of science fiction by reading novels and short stories. These were either printed in books or serialized in magazines.

Magazines have played a very important part in the history of science fiction. *Amazing Stories*, which began in 1926, was the first periodical devoted solely to tales of science fiction. For the next 30 years, during the "Golden Age" of science fiction, much of the groundbreaking work produced appeared in magazines. Magazines at that time were printed on cheap paper with rough edges. They were called "pulps." A few science fiction magazines still exist. Since the 1950s, however, most science fiction has been published in book form, both in paperback and hardcover.

Every year the World Science Fiction Society (WSFS) presents the Hugo Award, named after science fiction pioneer Hugo Gernsback. The award is presented to works of science fiction in several categories. But like the Oscars at the Academy Awards, the most important award is given out last. The WSFS awards its highest honor to the year's best novel.

Facing page: The cover of the March 1939 issue of *Amazing Stories*, featuring "The Raid from Mars." *Below:* A fan waits to have a book autographed at the 2005 63rd World Science Fiction Convention in Glasgow, Scotland.

Besides books and magazines, much printed science fiction today appears in fanzines. These are magazines written and produced by fans of science fiction. These fans are almost always unpaid amateurs who do it out of love for the genre. Fanzines, as well as personal websites and blogs, are a way for members of the science fiction fan community to communicate and publish their own creative works.

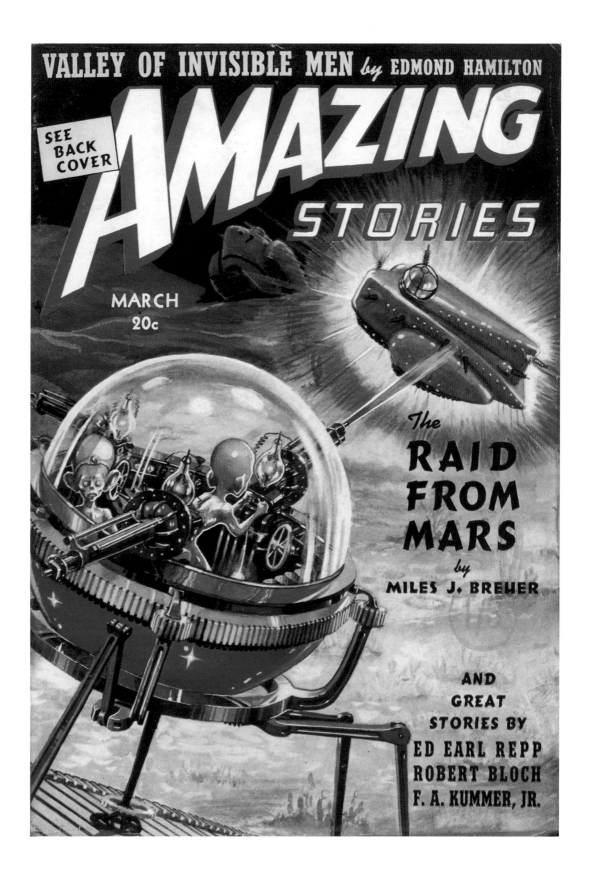

VALLEY OF INVISIBLE MEN *by* EDMOND HAMILTON

SEE BACK COVER

AMAZING
STORIES

MARCH
20c

The
RAID
FROM
MARS
by
MILES J. BREUER

AND
GREAT
STORIES BY
ED EARL REPP
ROBERT BLOCH
F. A. KUMMER, JR.

5

COMICS

Facing page: A collection of comic books featuring fantasy and science fiction.

Below: A page from an Alex Raymond-drawn *Flash Gordon* comic of the 1930s.

Buck Rogers in the 25th Century debuted as the world's first science fiction comic strip in August 1929. It was extremely popular, running continuously for 38 years in more than 400 newspapers around the world. It featured what people came to call "that Buck Rogers stuff": death rays, missiles, spaceships, robots, and more.

Flash Gordon started as a comic strip in 1934. First drawn by legendary comic artist Alex Raymond, the strip was created by King Features Syndicate in order to compete against the successful *Buck Rogers*. The strip featured adventurer Flash Gordon, his companion Dale Arden, and the brilliant Dr. Hans Zarkov, who crash-land on the planet Mongo and battle the evil forces of the tyrant Ming the Merciless.

Many comics featuring science fiction have appeared over the years. Some of the biggest names in science fiction have been published in comics, including authors Ray Bradbury and Edmond Hamilton. In the late 1930s and early 1940s, Hugo Gernsback published *Wonderland*, with art drawn by Frank R. Paul. *Planet Comics*, which appeared in the 1940s and early 1950s, featured space adventure stories with plots similar to *Flash Gordon* and *Buck Rogers*. *Weird Science* and *Weird Fantasy* were very popular comics of the early 1950s.

Superhero comics, like those published by DC Comics and Marvel, aren't technically considered science fiction. But these popular comics have many science fiction elements in them, such as space travel, robots, and aliens.

RADIO

Just as with comic strips, *Buck Rogers* and *Flash Gordon* were also science fiction pioneers in early radio programs. These were mainly adaptations of the comic strip stories, but radio brought the space adventure tales to a much wider audience.

Original science fiction programming was aired in the early 1950s on the *Dimension X* radio show. Unlike *Buck Rogers* and *Flash Gordon*, which were meant for kids, *Dimension X* was produced mainly for adults, with mature stories that challenged listeners. *Dimension X* lasted just one year, but in 1955 it was revived by NBC as *X Minus One,* keeping the same format and original programming. Respected authors such as Isaac Asimov, Robert Heinlein, Ray Bradbury, and Frederick Pohl had their stories adapted for the show. Many think *X Minus One* produced some of the finest radio dramas ever aired. It lasted until 1958, after 126 broadcasts.

The most famous science fiction radio show of all time was the October 30, 1938, adaptation of H. G. Wells' classic alien-invasion story, *The War of the Worlds*. The brainchild of actor/director Orson Welles, the CBS Radio and Mercury Theater production featured fake news reports, amazing sound effects, and on-the-spot reporting. Many people believed the broadcast was really happening. As many as one million people panicked, rushing into the streets and fleeing the cities to escape the "alien invasion."

Facing Page: Orson Welles during a broadcast of his CBS radio program.
Right: A man from Grovers Mill, New Jersey, stands ready with his trusty shotgun to ward off an attack by Martians after the 1938 radio presentation of *The War of the Worlds.*

Today, science fiction shows continue to be broadcast on radio, although not nearly as much as in years past. The British Broadcasting Corporation (BBC) has aired several modern science fiction programs, most famously *Doctor Who* and *The Hitchhiker's Guide to the Galaxy.*

TELEVISION

Facing page: Actor Frankie Thomas emerges from a spaceship hatch in an episode of *Tom Corbett–Space Cadet.*
Below: A poster for the first popular science fiction television show, *Captain Video and his Video Rangers.*

The first popular science fiction television series was *Captain Video and his Video Rangers.* The show aired on the American DuMont Network from 1949 until 1955. The show chronicled the adventures of Captain Video and his band of Video Rangers, who fought to bring justice throughout the solar system. Their headquarters was a secret base high on a mountaintop. The show was a live broadcast that ran five or six times each week. It had a very low budget (spacesuits resembled U.S. Army surplus uniforms), but it was extremely popular with kids and adults alike. Although many of the plots were simple, well-respected science fiction authors like Arthur C. Clarke and James Blish occasionally wrote episodes.

Tom Corbett–Space Cadet was a similar TV show that aired in the 1950s. Starring Frankie Thomas as Tom Corbett, the program followed the adventures of a group of Space Academy students training to become members of the Solar Guard, who were protectors of the solar system. Unlike many shows that would come later, *Tom Corbett–Space Cadet* was scientifically accurate, based on the information known in the 1950s, thanks to the insistence of Frankie Thomas and science advisor Willy Ley.

In the 1960s, science fiction television really took off, with such popular shows as *The Twilight Zone*, *The Outer Limits*, *The Invaders*, and the British import, *Doctor Who*. One man who struck it rich on the sci fi craze of the 60s was producer-director Irwin Allen. He had a string of hits that are some of the best-loved science fiction shows, even today: *Voyage to the Bottom of the Sea*, *The Time Tunnel*, *Land of the Giants*, and *Lost in Space*.

Born on June 12, 1916, Irwin Allen was a journalist, radio producer, and talent agent in the 1930s and 1940s. In the early 1950s, he produced his first film, the comedy *Double Dynamite*, starring Frank Sinatra and Groucho Marx. His documentary about undersea exploration, *The Sea Around Us*, was awarded the 1952 Oscar for Best Documentary Feature. In the 1970s, he would produce such blockbuster films as *The Towering Inferno*, and *The Poseidon Adventure*, which earned Allen the nickname, "The Master of Disaster."

In 1964, Allen brought *Voyage to the Bottom of the Sea* to television. Starring Richard Basehart as Admiral Nelson, and David Hedison as Captain Crane, skipper of the submarine *Seaview*, the show followed the adventures of the sub's crew as they battled evil-doers, undersea creatures, and even aliens. The show had a very popular following for four years, despite some outlandish episodes toward the end (including the infamous "Lobster Man" episode).

Irwin Allen's *Lost in Space* came to television in 1965. Of the four science fiction shows he brought to television, *Lost in Space* was Allen's "baby." The show centered on the Robinson family, who, along with friend Major Don West, blast off in the spaceship *Jupiter 2* to explore new planets. Unfortunately, their navigation system malfunctions, and they become hopelessly lost in space. As they try to find their way back to Earth, they explore new worlds and encounter strange aliens, most of them hostile. Also appearing are Dr. Zachary Smith, and Robot B-9, two of the most popular characters on the show.

Many people criticized Irwin Allen's television shows for not being scientifically accurate. In fact, many of the shows are just plain silly. But for a generation of kids and young adults who grew up watching *Lost in Space* or *Voyage to the Bottom of the Sea*, Allen's unique vision opened up a whole new world. Allen helped young fans capture a sense of wonder, which they would keep in later years as they explored the larger world of science fiction.

Irwin Allen continued making movies and television shows well into the 1970s and 1980s. He died November 2, 1991.

Above: The cover of the *Voyage to the Bottom of the Sea* season-one DVD collection.
Below: Robot B-9, Dr. Smith (Johnathan Harris), and Will Robinson (Billy Mumy), in *Lost in Space.*

On the night of September 8, 1966, NBC first aired *Star Trek*, a show that exploded like a photon torpedo onto the science fiction scene. The show followed the crew of the starship *Enterprise*, as they zoomed around the galaxy in the 23rd century, exploring strange new worlds and seeking out new life and new civilizations.

Star Trek boldly went where no television show had gone before: it was smart science fiction, optimistic in tone, with riveting stories by some of the most forward-thinking writers in the field. Equally important were the intriguing characters, including Captain James T. Kirk, the ship's brash and fearless commander, and Mr. Spock, the logical, pointy eared science officer from the planet Vulcan.

Above: Cast members of the original *Star Trek* series. Clockwise, from top left: Nichelle Nichols as Lieutenant Uhura; DeForest Kelley as Dr. McCoy; William Shatner as Captain James T. Kirk; and Leonard Nimoy as Mr. Spock.

The original *Star Trek* ran for only three seasons, for a total of 79 episodes, but fan support grew tremendously over the years. Loyal fans called themselves Trekkies (or Trekkers), and their support eventually led to ten feature films and five more live-action television shows, including *Star Trek: The Next Generation*, which ran for seven seasons in the 1980s and 1990s.

Star Trek was the creation of Gene Roddenberry. Born in El Paso, Texas, on August 19, 1921, Roddenberry spent his boyhood in Los Angeles, California. His father was a police officer. In college, Roddenberry first studied law, then aeronautical engineering. In World War II, he flew B-17 bombers against Japan. He flew 89 missions and was awarded the Distinguished Flying Cross and the Air Medal.

After the war, Roddenberry flew for Pan American World Airways, and then became a member of the Los Angeles Police Department for several years. He then started writing scripts for television, eventually becoming head writer for the highly popular Western, *Have Gun, Will Travel*. He also produced *The Lieutenant*, a show about the United States Marine Corps.

In 1964, Roddenberry had an idea for a new science fiction show. He called it *Star Trek*. Roddenberry wanted the show to be a kind of Western in outer space, with a spaceship crew exploring the wild frontier of the galaxy. He also compared *Star Trek* to the exploits of Horatio Hornblower, the fictional 19th-century British naval officer who made a career out of sailing the high seas and finding adventure on every distant horizon.

Above: Gene Roddenberry, creator of *Star Trek*.

Roddenberry shopped his idea around Hollywood, and was finally rewarded when Desilu Studios decided to let him produce the show. It aired on NBC for three years, starting in 1966, before low ratings forced the show's cancellation. Fan support for *Star Trek* was strong, however, and only increased as the show entered syndication, re-running on independent stations all across the country.

Roddenberry had an optimistic view of the future. He believed humanity would eventually overcome its troubles and then seek out its destiny among the stars. Affectionate fans nicknamed the creator of their beloved show, "The Great Bird of the Galaxy."

Below: Star Trek memorabilia on exhibit at the Science Fiction Museum in Seattle, Washington.

After *Star Trek* was canceled, Roddenberry kept busy developing other science fiction shows, such as *Genesis II*, and *The Questor Tapes*. When the *Star Trek* movies and *Star Trek: The Next Generation* series were produced in the 1980s and 1990s, they were led by Roddenberry's vision. Officially, he acted as executive consultant, but he was deeply involved with their creation.

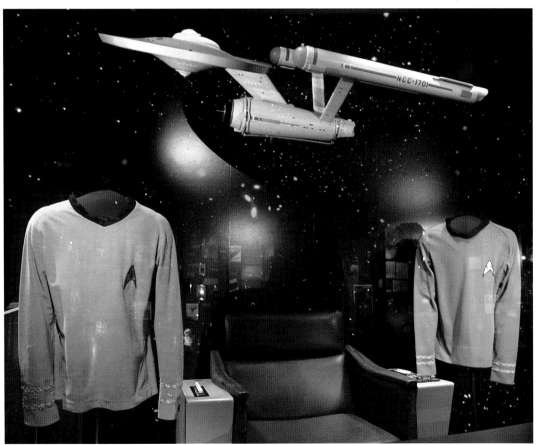

Gene Roddenberry, the man who brought so much joy and intelligence to science fiction television, died on October 24, 1991. After his death, a small container of his ashes was sent into space, where it orbited Earth for six years before burning up in the atmosphere. In his honor, a crater on Mars is named after him, as well as an asteroid, *4659 Roddenberry*.

Science fiction continues to be a major category of popular television. Action-oriented shows such as the original *Battlestar Galactica* have existed alongside brainier productions such as J. Michael Straczynski's *Babylon 5*, which won two Hugo Awards. Other popular shows have included *The X-Files*, *Farscape*, *Stargate SG-1*, and Joss Weden's *Firefly*. There is even a cable television channel, the Sci Fi Channel, devoted solely to science fiction. More recent productions, such as the remake of *Battlestar Galactica*, have won critical praise, and are very popular. Science fiction, it seems, has found a very good home on television, and is there to stay.

Below: The cast of characters from the hit television show, *Farscape*.

SCIENCE FICTION FILMS

Science fiction has been a popular film subject even during the medium's early days. In 1902, Paris magician Georges Méliès produced *A Trip to the Moon,* more than half a century before space travel became a reality. In 1927, German director Fritz Lang created the black-and-white silent classic, *Metropolis*, which depicted a futuristic world torn between two warring classes of society.

When sound was added to films in the late 1920s, and color in the 1940s and 1950s, film became an even more important outlet for science fiction. *Flash Gordon* and *Buck Rogers* came to the silver screen in the 1930s. After World War II, especially in the 1950s, people were scared of nuclear warfare, and the cinema reflected this fear. *The Day the Earth Stood Still*, *The Thing*, and *Invasion of the Body Snatchers* were very popular. Other important films from this decade included *Forbidden Planet* and *This Island Earth*.

The craft of creating realistic special effects, which gave so many science fiction films a wide-eyed sense of wonder, became more sophisticated. Ray Harryhausen is especially well-known for his amazing stop-motion animation, which combined models of creatures such as dinosaurs with real actors.

Harryhausen's models were photographed one frame at a time. After shooting each frame, he moved the creatures just a little bit. When the film was developed and then run through a projector at the normal speed of 24 frames per second, it looked as if the creatures were actually moving. Combined with real actors, the effect was thrilling to behold. It would be more than 25 years before Harryhausen's technique was made obsolete by computer-assisted animation.

Some of Ray Harryhausen's most famous science fiction films include *It Came From Beneath the Sea*, *The Beast from 20,000 Fathoms*, and *Valley of the Gwangi*.

Facing page: A theater lobby poster for *Flash Gordon Conquers the Universe*, starring Buster Crabbe as Flash Gordon. *Below:* Ray Harryhausen, master of animation.

12 New DYNAMIC CHAPTERS

THE New UNIVERSAL
Presents

FLASH GORDON
CONQUERS THE UNIVERSE

with

LARRY "Buster" CRABBE as FLASH GORDON
CAROL HUGHES as DALE ARDEN
ANNE GWYNNE as SONJA
CHARLES MIDDLETON as EMPEROR MING
FRANK SHANNON as DR. ZARKOV

Above: Ranger Bob flees in his canoe from the giant, radioactive mosquito in this scene from *Proboscis.*
Below: A terrifying scene from *Godzilla, King of the Monsters!*

Another popular theme of the 1950s science fiction cinema was the radioactive-mutant giant insect/lizard movie. These films reflected people's fears of the Cold War, atomic energy, toxic waste, or scientists meddling with nature. Some of the most popular nature-gone-wild films included *Them!* (giant mutant ants), *The Deadly Mantis* (a giant prehistoric praying mantis), *Tarantula* (a giant mutant spider), and the *Godzilla* films from Japan. This category remains popular even today, with examples such as *Eight Legged Freaks*, and the low-budget giant radioactive mosquito film, *Proboscis.*

There weren't as many science fiction films produced in the 1960s and early 1970s, but the ones that did get made were thoughtful and more artistic. Inventive films such as *2001: A Space Odyssey*, *Silent Running*, *Solaris*, and *Planet of the Apes*, laid the groundwork for science fiction being taken more seriously than in the past.

Two films, each released in 1977, had a huge impact on science fiction: *Star Wars* (later renamed *Star Wars: Episode IV – A New Hope*) and *Close Encounters of the Third Kind*.

Producer-director George Lucas got the idea for making *Star Wars* by watching serialized B-movies produced by the old Republic Pictures Corporation in the 1930s, such as *The Adventures of Captain Marvel*. Lucas wanted to make a science fiction movie with a similar flavor, but with a better story and higher production values for modern audiences.

George Lucas was born May 14, 1944, in Modesto, California. Growing up, he wasn't a very good student. He dreamed instead of becoming a racecar driver or auto mechanic. But a terrible auto accident soon after his high school graduation changed his life. His car rolled and struck a tree at a high speed. Lucas was thrown clear, and barely survived. As he recovered from his injuries, he decided to make something out of his life. "Well, I'm here," he said, "and every day now is an extra day. I've been given an extra day so I've got to make the most of it."

Lucas went to Modesto Junior College, then transferred to the University of Southern California's School of Cinema-Television in Los Angeles. He made several award-winning student films, including the science fiction thriller *THX 1138*, in which love and emotion are declared crimes.

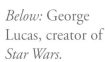

Below: George Lucas, creator of *Star Wars.*

After graduation, Lucas took several jobs as a cameraman or editor, barely staying afloat as he tried to convince a studio to make his movies. The style of his scripts was different from what most studio executives were used to—they were too confused to understand what Lucas was trying to accomplish. Lucas kept trying, never giving up on himself, or his belief in *Star Wars*. He knew that his "simple morality tale of good versus evil told across a fantastic landscape of exotic planets and bizarre creatures" would connect with audiences, if only he could get his film made.

After several years of knocking on doors and pounding the pavement, he got a studio executive interested in *Star Wars*, based on the success of *American Graffiti*, Lucas' 1973 film about early 1960s hot rod culture in Southern California.

Even during filming and editing, no one had much confidence that *Star Wars* would do well. Lucas refused to accept the limitations of special effects at the time, building his own visual effects company, Industrial Light & Magic (ILM), near his home outside of San Francisco. The special effects wizards at ILM created more than 300 effects shots for the film, setting a new standard in quality for science fiction films to come.

When it was released in 1977, *Star Wars* was a smash hit, much to everyone's surprise—everyone except George Lucas. He had never given up on himself, or his unique vision. The film broke all box office records, won eight Oscars, and launched five other films in the *Star Wars* saga.

To date, the *Star Wars* phenomenon—including film sequels, toy sales, books, etc.—has earned more than $20 billion worldwide, making it one of the most successful film franchises of all time. On June 9, 2005, the American Film Institute awarded Lucas its Lifetime Achievement Award.

Right: A scene from *Star Wars: Episode II – Attack of the Clones.* Left to right: Natalie Portman as Queen Amidala; R2-D2; and Hayden Christensen as Anakan Skywalker.

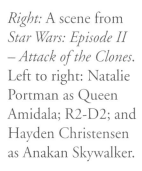

Above: Cast members of *Star Wars: Episode II – Attack of the Clones.* Left to right: Ewan McGregor as Obi-Wan Kenobi; Natalie Portman as Queen Amidala; and Hayden Christensen as Anakan Skywalker.

The same year *Star Wars* was released, another science fiction film burst onto the scene. *Close Encounters of the Third Kind* was director Steven Spielberg's second blockbuster hit, two years after the phenomenally successful *Jaws* in 1975. Today, Spielberg is one of the most successful and powerful directors in film history. He has been nominated for six Academy Awards for Best Director, winning twice.

Steven Spielberg was born on December 18, 1946, in Cincinnati, Ohio. He was raised in Scottsdale, Arizona, and Northern California. He was an Eagle Scout. He also loved to make action films with his friends using Super-8 film cameras. After high school, he attended college in Long Beach, California, and worked as an intern at Universal Studios in Los Angeles. At the young age of 22, he directed an episode of Rod Serling's *Night Gallery*.

After the incredible success of *Jaws*, Spielberg turned down the chance to direct *Jaws 2* and *Superman* in order to work on his pet project, a story about UFOs. He'd been fascinated by extraterrestrials since he was a boy, and had always wanted to write and direct a science fiction movie of his own.

Facing page: Filmmaker Steven Spielberg. *Below:* A theater lobby poster for Spielberg's 1982 science fiction masterpiece, *E.T. The Extra-Terrestrial.*

Close Encounters combined intense action with riveting characters. Typical of Spielberg's earlier films, it had a childlike sense of wonder. Departing from the hostile-alien films of the past, Spielberg's aliens were "good." It was a theme the director revisited with 1982's *E.T. The Extra-Terrestrial*, about a stranded alien who befriends a group of children who help him find his way "home." Spielberg considers *E.T.* to be his masterpiece.

Spielberg's science fiction films are noted for their groundbreaking visual effects. He is good friends with George Lucas. Spielberg's films frequently make use of Lucas' special effects studio, Industrial Light & Magic.

Spielberg went on to direct five more science fiction films: *Jurassic Park*, *The Lost World: Jurassic Park*, *A.I.: Artificial Intelligence*, *Minority Report*, and *War of the Worlds*.

Above: Los Angeles is devastated by a swarm of tornadoes in this scene from the 2004 film, *The Day After Tomorrow.*

Star Wars and *Close Encounters* had a great influence on future science fiction movies. Commercial success and public acceptance meant bigger budgets, A-list casts, and a chance to create more complex themes and stories. Special effects also became more and more advanced, especially with the introduction of digital filmmaking in the late 1990s and 2000s. Popular films that took advantage of these advances included *Independence Day*, *The Day After Tomorrow*, and *The Matrix* trilogy.

British director Ridley Scott produced two of the most influential and critically acclaimed science fiction films: *Alien*, the 1979 haunted-house-in-space story, and 1982's *Blade Runner*, based loosely on the groundbreaking novel by Philip K. Dick, *Do Androids Dream of Electric Sheep?*

Right: Filmmaker Ridley Scott directs a scene.

Academy Award winner James Cameron directed several important science fiction blockbusters. His action-packed films are very technically advanced, with eye-popping special effects. More importantly, the stories he directs are thoughtful, with recurring themes such as the impact of technology upon humankind. His science fiction films include *The Terminator*, *Aliens*, *The Abyss*, and *Terminator 2: Judgment Day*.

Above: A scene from *Aliens of the Deep.* *Below:* Director James Cameron on the set of *Aliens of the Deep.*

In 2005, Cameron produced *Aliens of the Deep*, a 3D film about a team of NASA scientists and marine biologists who go on a deep-ocean adventure. They discover strange sea creatures seldom seen by human eyes, alien life forms right here on Earth.

SCIENCE FICTION ART

Some emotions are very hard to communicate by written words alone. There are many awe-inspiring science fiction ideas that are best captured by visual communications. Science fiction got its start in literature, but as the genre became more popular, it naturally and swiftly moved to visual media as well, such as film and television. Drawn and painted art is another major outlet for science fiction.

Facing page: Heavy Time, by Don Maitz.
Below: Artist Don Maitz paints what he calls "fantastic realism."

Don Maitz has been an influential painter of science fiction and fantasy art for more than 25 years. His work reflects what he calls "fantastic realism." Maitz attended the Paier College of Art in Connecticut in the early 1970s, graduating at the top of his class. He eventually relocated to southern Florida, where he paints from his home-based art studio.

Maitz has painted covers and interior illustrations for many books and magazines, including *National Geographic,* Bantam Doubleday, and Random House Publishing. His book covers include works by Isaac Asimov, Ray Bradbury, and Allan Dean Foster.

Maitz's artwork has been featured in many museums across the country, and was included in NASA's 25th Anniversary presentation. He was a conceptual artist on the animated film, *Jimmy Neutron: Boy Genius,* and also worked on 2006's *Ant Bully.*

In 1990 and 1993, Don Maitz's imagination and attention to detail earned him two Hugo Awards, science fiction's highest honor.

GLOSSARY

ANDROID
A kind of robot that mimics people, both in appearance and behavior. In the film *Blade Runner*, based on Philip K. Dick's *Do Androids Dream of Electric Sheep?*, replicants are a type of android.

ARTIFICIAL INTELLIGENCE
A computer that is so advanced that it mimics human thought. Also referred to as AI.

B-MOVIE
A Hollywood motion picture originally meant to run as the second half of a double feature. B-movies were usually less flashy, with cheaper budgets, and were often genre films such as Westerns, horror, or science fiction.

CLONE
An organism that is "grown" from donor cells, making an exact copy of the original.

COLD WAR
The mainly diplomatic conflict waged between the United States and the former Soviet Union after World War II. The Cold War resulted in a large buildup of weapons and troops. It ended when the Soviet Union broke up in the late 1980s and early 1990s.

EXTRATERRESTRIAL
Something that comes from outside Earth or its atmosphere. In most science fiction stories, an extraterrestrial is a sentient alien from another planet.

GALAXY
A system of millions, or even hundreds of billions, of stars and planets, clustered together in a distinct shape, like a spiral or ellipse. Our Earth is located within the Milky Way Galaxy.

GENRE
A type, or kind, of a work of art. In literature, a genre is distinguished by a common subject, theme, or style. Some genres include science fiction, fantasy, and mystery.

HUGO AWARD
The annual award presented by the World Science Fiction Society to honor the year's best science fiction. The award is named after the legendary writer and editor Hugo Gernsback, who founded *Amazing Stories* (left) in 1926.

NASA
The National Aeronautics and Space Administration. NASA is the United States' main space agency, responsible for programs such as the Space Shuttle and unmanned space probes.

PERIODICAL
A newspaper or magazine that is published in regular intervals, such as daily or monthly. Much of the early science fiction of the 1930s and 1940s was published in periodicals, usually monthly magazines.

SOLAR SYSTEM
The collection of planets, asteroids, and comets that orbit the Sun. The solar system includes nine recognized planets: Mercury, Venus, Earth, Mars, Jupiter, Saturn, Uranus, Neptune, and Pluto.

UFO
An Unidentified Flying Object. In science fiction, a UFO is typically some kind of alien craft, such as a flying saucer.

INDEX

A

Abyss, The 27
Academy Awards 4, 24, 27
Adventures of Captain Marvel 21
A.I.: Artificial Intelligence 24
Alien 26
Aliens 27
Aliens of the Deep 27
Allen, Irwin 12, 13
Amazing Stories 4
American DuMont Network 10
American Film Institute 22
American Graffiti 22
Ant Bully 28
Arden, Dale 6
Asimov, Isaac 8, 28

B

Babylon 5 17
Bantam Doubleday 28
Basehart, Richard 13
Battlestar Galactica 17
Beast from 20,000 Fathoms, The 18
Blade Runner 26
Blish, James 10
Bradbury, Ray 6, 8, 28
British Broadcasting Corporation (BBC) 8
Buck Rogers in the 25th Century 6

C

California 22, 24
Cameron, James 27
Captain Video 10
Captain Video and his Video Rangers 10
CBS Radio 8
Cincinnati, OH 24
Clarke, Arthur C. 10
Close Encounters of the Third Kind 21, 22, 26
Cold War 20
Connecticut 28
Corbett, Tom 10
Crane, Captain 13

D

Day After Tomorrow, The 26
Day the Earth Stood Still, The 18
DC Comics 6
Deadly Mantis, The 20
Desilu Studios 16
Dick, Philip K. 26
Dimension X 8
Do Androids Dream of Electric Sheep? 26
Doctor Who 8, 12
Double Dynamite 12

E

Earth 13, 17, 27
Eight Legged Freaks 20
El Paso, TX 14
Enterprise 14
E.T. The Extra-Terrestrial 24

F

Farscape 17
Firefly 17
Flash Gordon 6, 8, 18
Florida 28
Forbidden Planet 18
Foster, Allan Dean 28
4659 Roddenberry 17
Frankenstein 4

G

Genesis II 16
Gernsback, Hugo 4, 6
Godzilla 20
Golden Age 4
Gordon, Flash 6, 8, 18

H

Hamilton, Edmond 6
Harryhausen, Ray 18
Have Gun, Will Travel 14
Hedison, David 13
Heinlein, Robert 8
Hitchhiker's Guide to the Galaxy, The 8
Hollywood, CA 16
Hornblower, Horatio 15
Hugo Award 4, 17, 28
Hyperion 4

I

Independence Day 26
Industrial Light & Magic (ILM) 22, 24
Invaders, The 12
Invasion of the Body Snatchers 18
It Came From Beneath the Sea 18

J

Japan 14, 20
Jaws 24
Jaws 2 24
Jimmy Neutron: Boy Genius 28
Jupiter 2 13
Jurassic Park 24

K

King Features Syndicate 6
Kirk, Captain James T. 14

L

Land of the Giants 12
Lang, Fritz 18
Ley, Willy 10
Lieutenant, The 14
Lifetime Achievement Award 22
"Lobster Man" 13
Long Beach, CA 24
Los Angeles, CA 14, 21, 24
Los Angeles Police Department 14
Lost in Space 12, 13
Lost World: Jurassic Park, The 24
Lucas, George 21, 22, 24

M

Maitz, Don 28

Mars 17
Marvel 6
Marx, Groucho 12
Matrix, The 26
Méliès, Georges 18
Mercury Theater 8
Metropolis 18
Ming the Merciless 6
Minority Report 24
Modesto, CA 21
Modesto Junior College 21
Mongo 6

N

NASA 27, 28
National Geographic 28
NBC 8, 14, 16
Nelson, Admiral 13
Night Gallery 24

O

Oscar 4, 13, 22
Outer Limits, The 12

P

Paier College of Art 28
Pan American World Airways 14
Paris, France 18
Paul, Frank R. 6
Planet Comics 6
Planet of the Apes 20
Pohl, Frederick 8
Poseidon Adventure, The 13
Proboscis 20

Q

Questor Tapes, The 16

R

Random House Publishing 28
Raymond, Alex 6
Republic Pictures Corporation 21
Robinson family 13
Robot B-9 13
Roddenberry, Gene 14, 15, 16, 17
Rogers, Buck 6, 8, 18

S

San Francisco, CA 22
School of Cinema-Television 21
Sci Fi Channel 17
Scott, Ridley 26
Scottsdale, AZ 24
Sea Around Us, The 12
Seaview 13
Serling, Rod 24
Shelly, Mary 4
Silent Running 20
Simmons, Dan 4
Sinatra, Frank 12
Smith, Dr. Zachary 13
Solar Guard 10
Solaris 20
Space Academy 10
Spielberg, Steven 24

Spock, Mr. 14
Star Trek 14, 15, 16
Star Trek: The Next Generation 14, 16
Stargate SG-1 17
Star Wars 21, 22, 24, 26
Star Wars: Episode IV – A New Hope 21
Straczynski, J. Michael 17
Superman 24

T

Tarantula 20
Terminator, The 27
Terminator 2: Judgement Day 27
Them! 20
Thing, The 18
This Island Earth 18
Thomas, Frankie 10
THX 1138 21
Time Machine, The 4
Time Tunnel, The 12
Tom Corbett–Space Cadet 10
Towering Inferno, The 13
Trip to the Moon, A 18
Twilight Zone, The 12
2001: A Space Odyssey 20

U

United States Army 10
United States Marine Corps 14
Universal Studios 24
University of Southern California 21

V

Valley of the Gwangi 18
Video Rangers 10
Voyage to the Bottom of the Sea 12, 13
Vulcan 14

W

War of the Worlds 24
War of the Worlds, The 8
Weden, Joss 17
Weird Fantasy 6
Weird Science 6
Wells, H. G. 4, 8
Welles, Orson 8
West, Major Don 13
Wonderland 6
World Science Fiction Society 4
World War II 14, 18

X

X-Files, The 17
X Minus One 8

Z

Zarkov, Dr. Hans 6